ideals
MOTHER'S DAY

When God brought forth this lovely one,
He chose these gifts of charm and grace—
A gentle voice, a tender touch,
A radiant smile on an earnest face.

He filled her days with unselfed love
That made of home a place to share;
She kept the fires of hearth and heart,
And spread our board with tasty fare.

As rays of light, her guiding thoughts
Enriched our world with spiritual good,
Imbued our lives with wisdom, love—
A masterpiece of motherhood.

Margaret E. McCaul

ISBN 0-8249-1018-4 350

IDEALS—Vol. 40, No. 3 March MCMLXXXIII IDEALS (ISSN 0019-137X) is published eight times a year,
February, March, April, June, August, September, November, December
by IDEALS PUBLISHING CORPORATION. 11315 Watertown Plank Road, Milwaukee, Wis. 53226
Second class postage paid at Milwaukee, Wisconsin. Copyright © MCMLXXXIII by IDEALS PUBLISHING CORPORATION.
POSTMASTER: Send address changes to Ideals, Post Office Box 2100, Milwaukee, Wis. 53201
All rights reserved. Title IDEALS registered U.S. Patent Office.
Published simultaneously in Canada.

ONE YEAR SUBSCRIPTION—eight consecutive issues as published—$15.95
TWO YEAR SUBSCRIPTION—sixteen consecutive issues as published—$27.95
SINGLE ISSUE—$3.50

The cover and entire contents of IDEALS are fully protected by copyright and must
not be reproduced in any manner whatsoever. Printed and bound in U.S.A.

Publisher, James A. Kuse
Editor/Ideals, Colleen Callahan Gonring
Associate Editor, Linda Robinson
Production Manager, Mark Brunner
Photographic Editor, Gerald Koser
Copy Editor, Barbara Nevid
Art Editor, Duane Weaver

The Home-Maker

"To keep a house and cook and tend and sew
Is wasting all one's talent," wistfully she said.

Along the windowsill her houseplants grow,
With finest loaves her family is fed,
And in her yard her sun-sweet linens blow.

Her caring neighbors daily tread
The path that finds her door where heartsease grows,
And where her wisdom is their minds' bread.

Within this home her little boy is free
To bring his friends or pets or fishing line
To share with her. "My mommy's good to me,"
He whispered once with boyish eyes ashine.

There is no recompense in muse or art
To equal love in child's or neighbor's heart.

Ruth M. Rasey

It Is May

The snow is gone, and fragrance fills the air,
And all the earth is chanting, "It is May."
The iris and the lilies bloom today
Where only yesterday the soil was bare.

Dame Nature scatters beauty everywhere.
Forgotten are the days that were so gray.
The snow is gone, and fragrance fills the air,
And all the earth is chanting, "It is May."

The feathered warblers chirp a morning prayer
As they flit back and forth in bright array;
Then trees and flowers join the roundelay.
The glory of the Lord they all declare.
The snow is gone, and fragrance fills the air,
And all the earth is chanting, "It is May."

Pearle Lange Schuler

A Mother's Song

My little unborn child, I carry you
Without your yes or no to life and light.
Would you consent, I wonder, to be born
If you could choose and know each grief, each plight
We all endure who walk the mortal road?
Would you consent to share the human load?

I think you would; you are so close, so close
These many months to one rejoicing heart,
You cannot help but feel how strong, how sweet
A joy can be, and long to claim your part
In such a heritage which life bestows
To more than compensate for all the woes.

I know you would; for I can promise you
The wonder of the stars, the seas, the hills,
The miracle of love and comradeship,
The breathless sum of loveliness which fills
Our world. O small, new soul that looks toward birth,
I bring you to a good, a glorious earth.

                                        Hester Suthers

Grace V. Watkins

Grace V. Watkins was born in Fargo, North Dakota. She graduated from Jamestown College in North Dakota and later from the University of Iowa. She taught at various colleges throughout the Midwest, a vocation she truly enjoyed. Miss Watkins' poetry first appeared in *Ideals* in 1952. She has also written for many other publications such as *Musical America, Etude,* and various church periodicals. Another gratifying pastime is helping others with their writing careers. Grace Watkins' poetry reflects her basic values and beliefs by means of her customary themes of family, religion, and nature. She presently resides in a retirement home and derives pleasure from the many contacts and activities she is experiencing. She also finds satisfaction in writing poetry by request for others to enjoy.

For My Mother

My mother's love is larkspur,
Blue and sweet,
The gentle wind
Along a quiet street.
My mother's love
Is little silver singing
Of twilight bells,
The soft and soundless winging
Of birds in flight
Across an evening sky,
The first star, hushed
And gold and high;
And on all pathways,
Whether joy or grief,
The clear unwavering
Candle of belief.

A Happy Day

Any day is a happy day
If you have watched a bluebird fly
From branches of a tall green elm
Into the shining azure sky.

Any day is a happy day
If you have seen a sun-bright flower
And said a prayer of thankfulness
For God's abundant peace and power.

Any day is a happy day
If you have helped someone to share
The lifting love of God and to say
A hushed and holy prayer.

For Mother's Day

My mother taught my heart to see
A velvet-coated bumblebee.
My mother taught my heart to know
Allegro-singing winds that blow,
To find a daisy field as fair
As pages from a book of prayer,
And always when I walk the sod,
To walk a chapel aisle to God.

Memo for a Spring Day

Make friends with a honeysuckle wind;
Be a cousin to meadow sun,
A comrade to green, sky-facing hills
Where sparkling rivers run.
Go find an elm where a cardinal bird
Is playing his tiny flute.
Lift up your arms, lift up your voice,
And answer his bright salute,
Filled with songs of gladness that sing
To the God who made the glories of spring.

Mother's Day

More beautiful than May-bright skies,
Than hills where golden sunshine lies,
Is love within a mother's eyes.

Softer than dawn across the land,
Than little waves against the sand
Is healing of a mother's hand.

And oh, more largo-sweet and fair
Than chapel bells in twilight air
Is music of a mother's prayer.

My Mother

My mother loved the quiet things—a wind
Across a field of summer-golden wheat,
Andante waves that murmur on the sand,
A child's soft vesper prayer, viola-sweet.

She loved the lovely things—rain in the night,
The rose-and-silver promise of the dawn,
The sound of migratory birds in flight,
And crocus blossoms when the snow is gone.

And oh, she loved the holy things—a psalm,
A sanctuary warm with faith and prayer,
And organ music singing through the calm
Of twilight time, serene and largo-fair.

Because she taught my heart to love these things,
The days go by on wonder-lighted wings.

Lilacs

Spring brings the lilacs
To a little girl
Gathering their flowers
In a happy world.
Two little hands enshrine them
In each room,
Loved flowers of purple
And perfume.

Spring brings the lilacs
To a maiden fair
Who, weaving purple lilacs
In her hair,
Walks with her love
In promise old yet new,
Henceforth remembering lilacs
Wet with dew.

Springs bring the lilacs
Back and back again;
Youth and old age inhale
Their sweet incense.
Memory lives
And is a precious thing
When lilacs bring their glory
To the spring.

Essie L. Mariner

When Lilacs Bloom

Oh, to be home when the lilacs bloom,
To feel the spring breeze and smell their perfume,
The blossoms all sparkly in the morning dew,
And the sky up above such a heavenly blue.

Lilacs always remind me of home,
When as a child through the woods I'd roam;
I'd wade the cool waters of the little creek
And feel the warm sun as it touched my cheek.

I remember the nights in the pale moonlight,
And the lilacs would glow all purple and white.
I'd look out my window to the scene below,
In those days when the lilacs bloomed, long ago.

Joyce Suter Whitcomb

A mother loves
The gentle breeze
That whispers in
The willow trees.
She loves the hills,
The winding path,
And hearing little
Children laugh.

What Mother Loves

Alice Leedy Mason

A mother loves
All newborn things—
The colt, the pup;
Their presence brings
An understanding,
Tenderness,
And hands that touch
With gentleness.

A mother loves
Unusual sights;
A rainbow after rain
Delights;
A shooting star,
The lightning's source—
She knows where violets bloom,
Of course.

A mother loves
The quiet time,
Books to share
In prose and rhyme,
Kittens chasing
Butterflies,
And clouds that clutter up
The skies.

These are the things
That make life real;
The sound of bells,
How strangers feel,
A deer in flight,
The wild bird's call—
A mother knows
And loves them all.

The Greatest Gift

The world is such a wondrous place
With all its many-patterned lace—
The silhouettes of stately pine
Against a sunset borderline,
The purple mountains just below,
The mirrored streams which gaily flow
Through meadowlands, the orchards, too,
Ah, yes, each thing within our view,
Be it an ocean wide and deep
Or just a rose that wakes from sleep.
And I would thank the God above
For all his kindness and his love
In sending us these things so fair.
But what, I ask you, can compare
With this, the greatest gift God planned—
A mother—ah, so sweet, so grand!

Phyllis C. Michael

Morning Song

The white church dozes in the morning sun,
Warm with the charm of budding May.
It welcomes people as they come,
Through meadows green with new, sweet hay.
Contentment dwells where the white church keeps
A fragrant tryst with Maytime's bliss;
They drowse where lovely orchards lie
Aroused by springtime's waking kiss.

Brian F. King

May Is Here

The skies are silvery gray and low;
The soft wind sweeps the gentle rain;
And tulips burst in clouds of red,
For May, sweet May, is here again.

The showers are quickly o'er,
And as the sun comes shining through,
I walk along the garden path
When everything is fresh and new.

I like to dig in clean wet sand
Or pull a weed or sprig of grass
And set a flower out here and there
Or watch the brilliant redbird pass.

I see the squirrel nimbly leap
From limb to limb in a tree;
The birds drop down upon the lawn
To grab a bug I cannot see.

Out near the birdbath by the wall,
The air is filled with sunshine pure;
The mourning dove coos to its mate—
No other month's like May, I'm sure.

We are not tuned for noise and such;
Our country life is quiet here.
We listen to the music of the birds
And know that God is near.

Gertrude Bryson Holman

Topsy Turvy

I rush to town to purchase bread
And hurry home with cake instead;
I give the space I need for rows
Of corn and beans to golden glows;
I buy a bonnet, Quaker-prim,
And pin a poppy on its brim,
Aware that poppies have the skill
To garnish primness with a frill.

I squeeze my toes in shoes that bind
And run, barefooted, through my mind;
I tuck my hair back carefully
And beg the wind to set it free;
I train my hands for stove and sink
And paint my nails a primrose pink,
For something in me, April-wild,
Refuses to be clipped and filed.

I choose such words as *must* and *will,*
And idle on a summer hill;
I wind my watch, a slave to time,
And waste a furlough on a rhyme;
Averse to fact, immune to fiction,
My self becomes a contradiction—
A topsy-turvy lass am I,
In love with earth and sea and sky!

Vivian Laramore Rader

The Homing Heart

Each morning little roadways beckon me
To leave housewifely chores undone,
Forsake such homely tasks as brewing tea
And baking muffin, tart or bun.

At times I follow some lane's crooked finger;
I leave the bed unmade, the floor
Unswept, the dishes stacked—scarce do I linger
To close the blind or lock the door.

All day I roam, held in the witching thrall
Of my roadway-seducer. Where
Sun-dappled woodlands slope, I hear the call
Of some lone quail, and to his lair

I chase a frightened squirrel. Then, on straw
Which thickly mats the earth-sweet sod,
I lie and listen to an insect draw
His bow and hymn a tune to God.

At last the woods grows dim; the sun drops low.
I feel the chilling damp of dew,
And quick, on swift-winged, homesick feet, I go
Straight back to my wee house and you!

Winnie Lynch Rockett

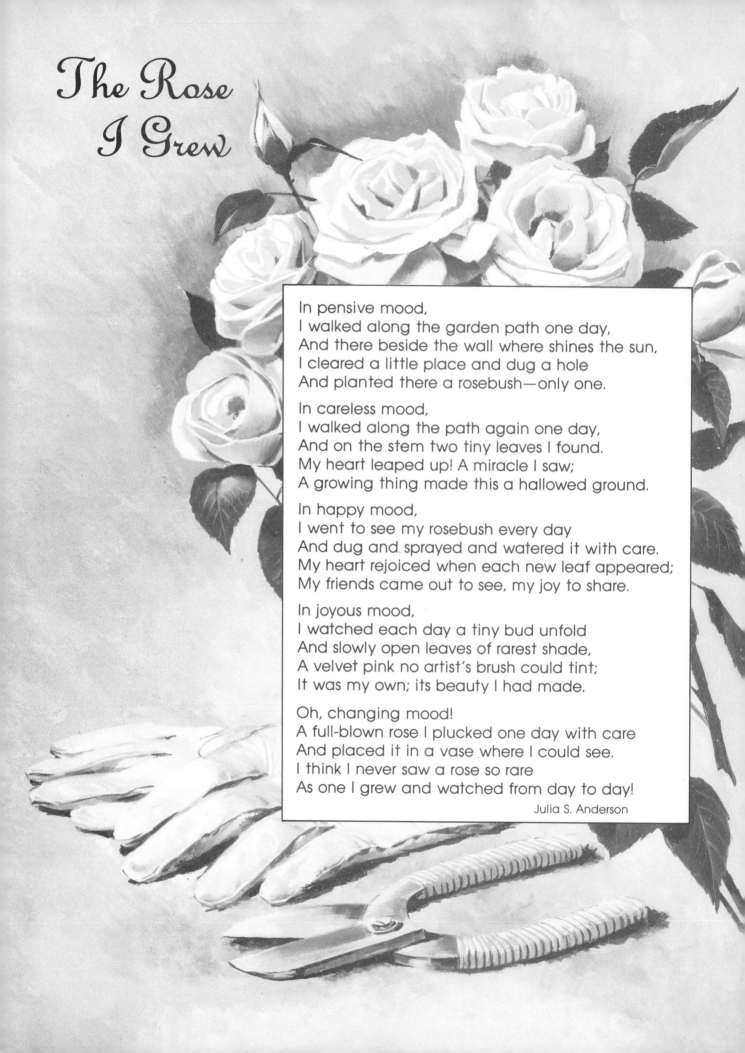

The Rose I Grew

In pensive mood,
I walked along the garden path one day,
And there beside the wall where shines the sun,
I cleared a little place and dug a hole
And planted there a rosebush—only one.

In careless mood,
I walked along the path again one day,
And on the stem two tiny leaves I found.
My heart leaped up! A miracle I saw;
A growing thing made this a hallowed ground.

In happy mood,
I went to see my rosebush every day
And dug and sprayed and watered it with care.
My heart rejoiced when each new leaf appeared;
My friends came out to see, my joy to share.

In joyous mood,
I watched each day a tiny bud unfold
And slowly open leaves of rarest shade,
A velvet pink no artist's brush could tint;
It was my own; its beauty I had made.

Oh, changing mood!
A full-blown rose I plucked one day with care
And placed it in a vase where I could see.
I think I never saw a rose so rare
As one I grew and watched from day to day!

Julia S. Anderson

Old-Fashioned Gardens

Where have all the gardens gone
That grew old-fashioned flowers?
The flowers that Grandma loved so well,
In half-forgotten bowers—
Sweet William, mignonette so sweet,
Primroses row on row,
A flash of yellow buttercups,
Sweet snowdrops in the snow.

These dear old-fashioned flowers hold
Fond memories that last,
For they bring back a vision of
Sweet gardens of the past
With lovely ladies strolling down
A garden path so fair
While sweet old-fashioned flowers sent
Their fragrance through the air.

Carice Williams

Family
Tree

In the center of life's garden,
A mother gently sows
A special seed, a seed of love,
That sprouts, then grows and grows.
From day to day, from year to year,
She nurtures it with care,
Yet, understanding of its needs,
She gives it room and air.
Through winter and through summer,
Through sun and rain-filled hours,
The seedling reaches upward;
It branches, and it flowers.
In the center of life's garden
Grows a thing of majesty,
Rooted well with mother's love—
A blessed family tree!

Alice Joyce Davidson

Mother in a Garden

She plants the phlox and marigolds
And tends them in a lovely bed;
She prunes the rose and sees it climb
With yellow blossoms overhead.

This is a happy place for her
To feel the sun upon her brow,
To mingle with the mockingbird
And pick a lilac from the bough.

Her life is like the fragrant buds
Uplifting with a constant cheer;
Her heart is fresh with blooms of love
She scatters daily everywhere.

Inez Franck

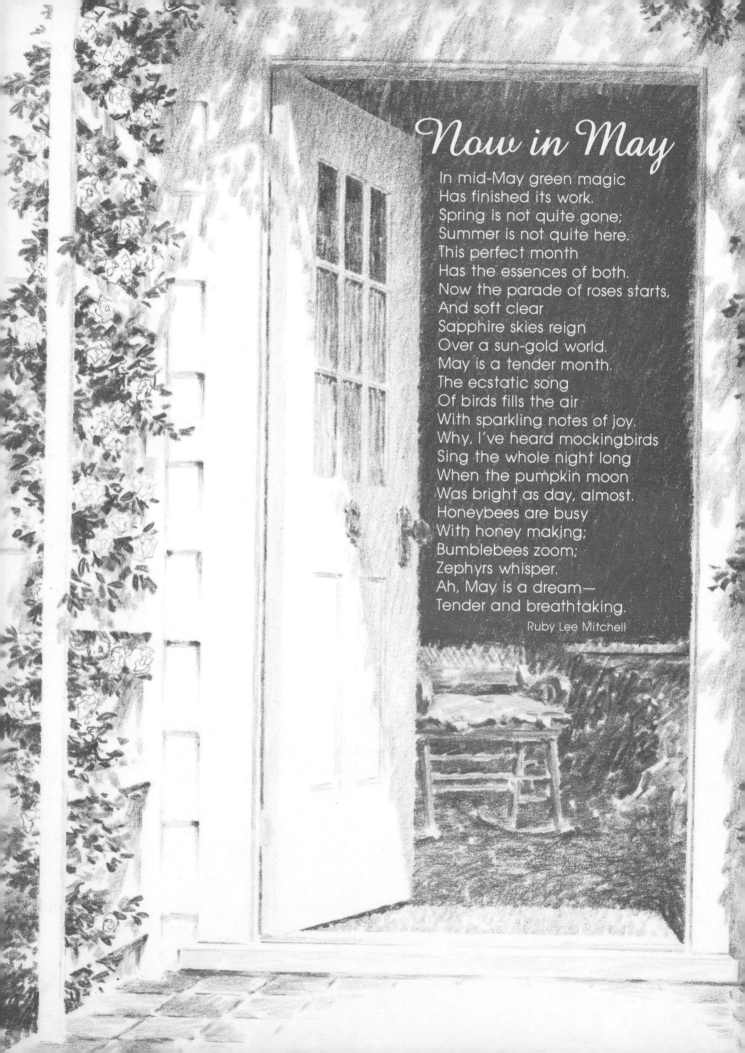

Now in May

In mid-May green magic
Has finished its work.
Spring is not quite gone;
Summer is not quite here.
This perfect month
Has the essences of both.
Now the parade of roses starts,
And soft clear
Sapphire skies reign
Over a sun-gold world.
May is a tender month.
The ecstatic song
Of birds fills the air
With sparkling notes of joy.
Why, I've heard mockingbirds
Sing the whole night long
When the pumpkin moon
Was bright as day, almost.
Honeybees are busy
With honey making;
Bumblebees zoom;
Zephyrs whisper.
Ah, May is a dream—
Tender and breathtaking.

Ruby Lee Mitchell

FENCE LINES

The house in which I grew up had a ragged old fence when we moved in. Mother declared that the first order of business was to put up a new fence—a good, strong picket fence.

Now a picket fence offers a wonderful chance to display originality and personality; I mean, pickets can be wide or narrow, tall or short, square or pointed, straight or tapered, plain or fancy—there are endless variations. Mother always made the aesthetic decisions for the family, and she unimaginatively chose to use one-by-four pickets, three-and-a-half feet high, straight-sided with square tops.

I wasn't old enough to handle a prominent, major job like putting up a fence, and Dad was more of a workbench putterer; so we hired a professional. A real carpenter came with a load of the cleanest, straightest lumber I'd ever seen, and in a couple of days we had the most beautiful fence in the neighborhood.

Dad was appointed to sand any rough edges and cover the fence with two coats of paint. But after that I was the one who wielded the brush every time the fence needed new paint— quite a few times over the years. I never did pull off a "Tom Sawyer" though. My friends all vanished like snow in May when painting time came around.

One thing about layers of paint on a picket fence—as more coats were applied (different colors, of course), the smoother and rounder the picket tops became. Of course, this was easier on the children's clothes when they climbed over the fence (gates were too slow). Eventually Mother could lean on it comfortably while she swapped recipes and gossip with the neighbors.

Dad used the fence for tying up his tomatoes and sunflowers. It was also handy to loop the dog's leash around a picket while I was playing kick-the-can or baseball.

Despite all the loving care that fence received from me, it proved to be hurtful to me one time. I was walking along the tops of the pickets, tightrope fashion, when I slipped and fell, straddling the fence. A very embarassed young man then had to submit to maternal first aid!

I visited the old neighborhood the other day, and I must say that fence is still holding up well. Mother's gone now, but if she had been there, she would probably have inspected the fence closely and said, "I think it's time to paint the fence again—maybe a nice cream color this time. What do you think?"

Donald S. Henning

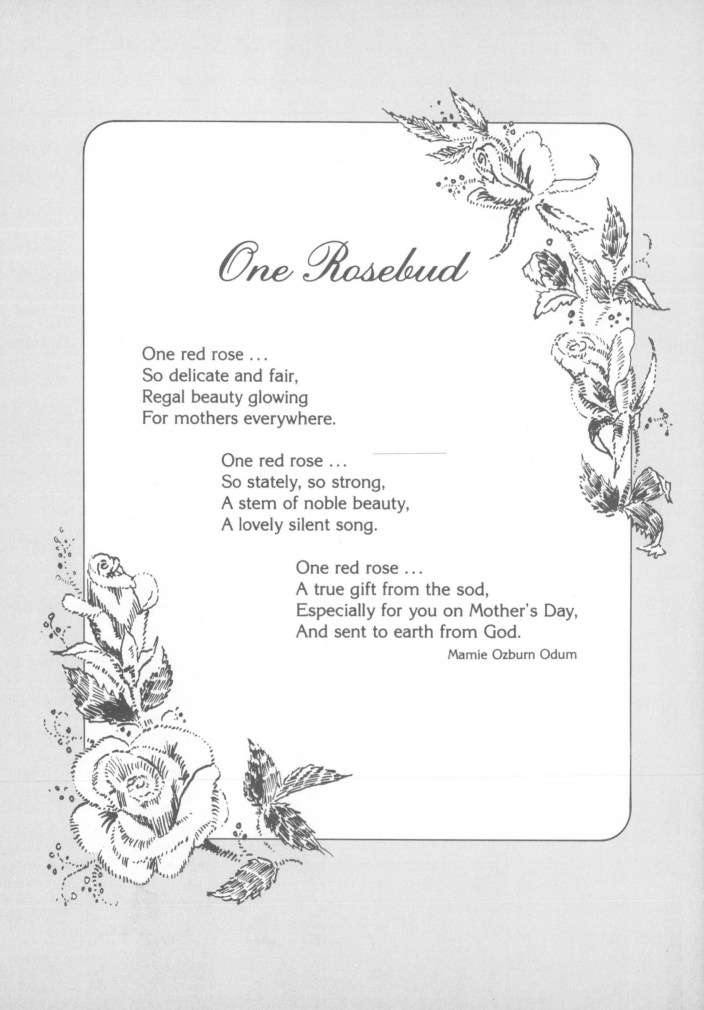

One Rosebud

One red rose …
So delicate and fair,
Regal beauty glowing
For mothers everywhere.

One red rose …
So stately, so strong,
A stem of noble beauty,
A lovely silent song.

One red rose …
A true gift from the sod,
Especially for you on Mother's Day,
And sent to earth from God.

Mamie Ozburn Odum

My Kitchen

My favorite room in all the house
Where I prefer to be
Is in my kitchen, friendly, bright,
Where I cook happily.
It's here I test new recipes;
From here sweet scents arise,
That drift about the neighborhood,
Of fresh baked bread and pies.
Here friends informally drop in
And chatter merrily,
And here a dream is often born
O'er cakes and cups of tea.
'Tis here you'll find me after dark
Beside the kitchen sink
As through the window I look out
At stars that nod and wink.
It's always cozy in this spot
For family or guest;
Of all the rooms within my house,
I like my kitchen best.

Carice Williams

Greatest Gift

Each time I rise and see the glorious morning,
The rosy sun, the fresh and sparkling dew,
The baby's crib where dawn comes slowly creeping,
And hear soft sounds below, I know that you
Have tiptoed downstairs to your waiting kitchen,
Have spread a checkered tablecloth, ironed sweet,
And set the cups and saucers brightly gleaming;
I know my world could not be more complete.
I shave and sing into my mirror;
The spice of baking wafts up the stairs,
And in this paradise you keep so lovely,
I pause and say a deeply thankful prayer.

Dan A. Hoover

Mayflowering

Come with me a-Mayflowering
In the wood and field.
We'll gather up the beauty
That spring and nature yield.

We'll find sweet, white daisies
Which hold a ray of sun,
And a delicate, lacy fern,
The graceful, airy one,

Or dainty lady's slippers
In their pink gowns,
Violets of many hues,
Bloodroot's starry crown.

How lovely is our May bouquet
In purple, white, and gold!
We've brought spring to our homes today,
And with it, joys untold.

Marcy Spicer

Seasonal Thoughts
Mother's Day

Within the corner of my heart
I've safely tucked away
A sweet bouquet of memories
From happy bygone days,
And there within each memory
I see your smiling face—
Dear Mother, you're a flower
That time will never fade.

Loise Pinkerton Fritz

No language can express
The power and beauty
And heroism
Of a mother's love.

Edwin H. Chapin

There is no velvet so soft
As Mother's lap,
No rose so lovely
As her smile,
No path so flowery
As that imprinted
With her footsteps.

Archbishop Thomson

Love in a home is like a lamp
Around whose steady glow
The children gather safe and warm
Though storms outside may blow.

And in the shadowy years to come,
The children long since grown
Will light love's lamps in other homes
For children of their own.

Barbara Dolliver

A time for the fruiting of plum trees,
A leafing time, too, for the rose,
A time for the calling of neighbors
Across the new-sprouting hedgerows,

A time for the planting of zinnias,
I'll put a new rose cutting here;
A time to show faith by our planting—
'Tis spring then each day of the year.

Minnie Roberts Dreesen

April is a laundress
Mixing silver suds
To rinse the lacy dance frocks
Of apple-blossom buds.

May Day is the nursemaid
Who looks the flowers over
And ties the little bonnets
On the buttercup and clover.
                    Anne Robinson

For when you looked
Into my mother's eyes,
You knew, as if He had told you,
Why God sent her
Into the world.
It was to open
The minds of all
Who looked,
To beautiful thoughts.
                    James M. Barrie

It is the candle turn of day
When children leave their outdoor play
And father's eager homing feet
Make welcome echoes up the street.
It is the hour when mothers spread
A table with the evening bread,
When lamps are lighted on the walls
And evening's benediction falls.
                    Marguerite Gode

The angels come and loving vigil keep
Beside your bed as Mother dims the light;
Then baby moonbeams kiss your eyes to sleep
And drop a dream into your crib tonight.
                    Mary Fink

The sweetest sounds
To mortals given
Are heard in mother,
Home, and heaven.
                    William Goldsmith Brown

Today, I
Read a book,
Listened to a secret,
Looked at a bug,
Squeezed a hand,
Wiped a nose.
And I

Settled an argument,
Kissed a hurt,
Cleaned a milk spill,
Drilled a spelling lesson,
Mended a rip.
Oh, yes, I also

Heard a secret,
Zipped a jacket,
Smiled away a tear,
Explained a problem,
Shared in a prayer;

For I'm
Just a mother.
                    Lorraine M. Halli

My Flower

My child,
You are to me
Like a tiny flower
Which reaches its petals
To the sun
For warmth and light.
You reach to me
For love and life

Like the roots
Which grope through earth
For water.
You feed on my mind
For all that you wonder.

And as the sun rests
And her petals close,
You nestle to my breast
Like a gentle rose.

Emily M. Welch

Mother's Work

Mother's arms were made for holding,
Made for enfolding snug and tight
Little forms so soft and helpless
Nestled there to say good night.

Mother's hands were made for stroking,
Made for soothing childish woes;
Balm of wondrous magic healing
Through each gentle finger flows.

Mother's lips were made for kissing,
Made for drowning childish fears;
Smiles and kisses both together
Stop the flow of bitter tears.

Mother's heart was made for loving,
Made for love no others know.
God in heaven, bless and keep it
Ever pure as whitest snow.

Cora Lindsey Field

A Good Mother

A good mother is the loving foundation upon which the home is built, the guardian of the small lives she has borne. Tenderly she nurtures the precious souls entrusted to her care, gratefully thanking God for the individual beauty, personality, and talents of each child and humbly praying for the wisdom and understanding to help each attain a sense of his own self-worth and special niche in God's wondrous world.

A good mother is the first and most loving teacher that the child will ever know, the most soothing nurse that will ever attend him, and his most understanding judge on earth. A good mother is her child's dearest and most faithful friend. He is always in her heart and mind, and she never ceases to sacrifice, work, and pray for what is best for him. A good mother is a shining beacon on the sea of life.

Louise Pugh Corder

When Edith was a little girl
Of maybe three or four,
Her father found a kitten
On the walk right near his store.
Her fur was black, her eyes were green,
And she was soft as silk;
And he brought her home for dinner
And a dish of nice warm milk.

And Edith loved that little cat
For many, many years,
And when it finally went away,
Her eyes were filled with tears.

When Edith was a teenage girl
And fine fashions were her dream,
She had a cat that matched her room
Of beige and brown and cream.
Just a furry little calico
That slept right on her bed,
With paws like her furniture
And a coat just like her spread.

And Edith loved that little cat
All through her teenage years,
And when it finally went away,
Her eyes were filled with tears.

When Edith was a married girl
And her children were her pleasure,
She had a cat with golden fur
Who was the family treasure.
And when the children grew and left
And traveled far and wide,
Her furry, golden pussycat
Remained right by her side.

And Edith loved that little cat
Who helped her calm her fears,
And when it finally went away,
Her eyes were filled with tears.

When Edith became an older girl
And her hair was turning gray,
She had a silver pussycat
That was just a little stray.
It loved to sit by the fireside
Or in the nice warm sun,
And it curled right up beside her
When the day was finally done.

And Edith loved that little cat
All through those silver years,
And when it finally went away,
Her eyes were filled with tears.

Edith
Loved
That Little Cat

Now Edith is a grandmother,
And her hair is streaked with snow,
And she has a pure white pussycat
As everyone must know.
And her days are spent just petting her
And dreaming of before
And all the kittens she has had
Since she's been three or four.

And Edith loved those little cats
And their friendship through the years
And the many smiles that they brought
Which far outnumbered tears.

Dr. Donald R. Stoltz, President
Norman Rockwell Museum
Philadelphia, Pennsylvania

A Little Boy

His feet will always find a puddle;
His knees must rest in dirt.
And though you've changed it twice today,
He may need another shirt.

His hands alone don't show the grime,
But also cheeks and chin.
He'll never know his sparkling eyes
Reveal the mischief he's been in!

But when you tuck him in at night
And after prayers are said,
No greater joy than this—to see
Pure innocence asleep in bed.

JoAnn Dunne

A Little Girl

Her feet love to wear new patent shoes
And to dance and skip at play.
She also knows to stomp just one
When she doesn't get her way.

Her hands may rock a baby doll,
Or mix and bake mud pies.
They love to go through Mommy's purse
In search of some great surprise.

She really is an imp at times,
Much to your displeasure;
But giggles, smiles, and angel eyes
All bring more love than you could measure.

JoAnn Dunne

Pattern for Spring

Spring is every lovely flower—
Apple blossoms pink and white,
Purple violets in a glen,
Forsythia blooming golden-bright.

Spring is water—brooks that sing,
The soft adagio of rain,
Small puddles that reflect the sky,
Wet lilacs in a country lane.

Spring is children skipping rope,
Playing marbles in the sun,
Making dandelion chains,
Quiet sleep when day is done.

Spring is the little twilight prayer
You quietly say to God above,
Assured that He is listening
To every word with shoreless love.

All of the lovely thoughts that sing
Within your heart, all these are spring.

Grace V. Watkins

Breakfast

Two forks, two spoons, two knives,
Coffee perking, bacon frying,
The breakfasts of our life beginning
Midst promises of love undying.

Three forks, three spoons, three knives,
Three heads are bowed for grace.
An impish cherub, golden haired,
In our hearts now fills a place.

Four forks, four spoons, four knives,
A happy hubbub starts our day.
Four voices blend in breakfast chatter,
Then off to work and school and play.

Off to work and school and play,
Breakfasts pass, and children grow.
The little birds must make new nests;
Breakfasts pass, and children go.

Each day still dawns with promise new,
And breakfast starts our daily lives.
But it's quieter now at breakfast time—
Two forks, two spoons, two knives.

Anna Jean Allen

My parents never said, "Child, run out and play.
We've a thousand things to do today."
They took time to look at the many things
That happiness to a small child brings.

Wonders to Share

Together we watched the hummingbird gather
Nectar from flowers, then light as a feather
Dart up and away, to come again
Another day.

They took time to tell of the great out-of-doors,
About which all parents know;
Chores were forgotten, for in their wise ways,
They helped a young mind to grow.

Together we'd find a bright butterfly
Or a dogtooth violet in May;
Watch a spider spin its silvery web
Neath the eaves on a summer day,

Or walk in the meadow where the first bobolink
Sang a happy song in its flight;
And we'd mimic the cry of the whippoorwill
That called in the shadows of night.

A lifetime of love to remember,
Of childhood days happy and free,
A heritage of wonders shared—
All these my parents gave to me.

Angie Davidson Bass

A Mother's Prayer --

Dear Father who art in heaven

You give me a glimpse of heaven in those special tender moments of motherhood.

Hallowed be Thy Name, Thy kingdom come

Help me as I strive to create a corner of your kingdom right here with harmony in our home.

Thy will be done

Let all I do be an inspiration for my children to follow You.

Give us this day our daily bread

Keep me ever thankful for the warmth that makes each loaf rise and aware of the love that keeps warmth in our home.

And forgive us our trespasses

Forgive me, Lord. Forgive me, children ... Through all the years, through all the tears, I'm deeply sorry for the many times I may have hurt you ... I did not mean to ... I'm even sorrier for the many times I may not have let you know how much I love you.

As we forgive others

lifting the love displayed wordlessly by an unselfish act ... forgetting the trivial hurts.

Lead us not into temptation

from all that awaits as we venture into the world beyond our fence.

But deliver us from evil

Protect the children so precious while I await their safe return.

For Thine is the kingdom

Make me worthy of it ... a better mother, more loving and more lovable.

And the power and the glory

The joy of knowing You love me, a mother, because I am your child ... as I love my children because I am their mother.

Forever

Thank You for the miracles that made me both your child and their mother.

Amen

Mary-Alice Wightman

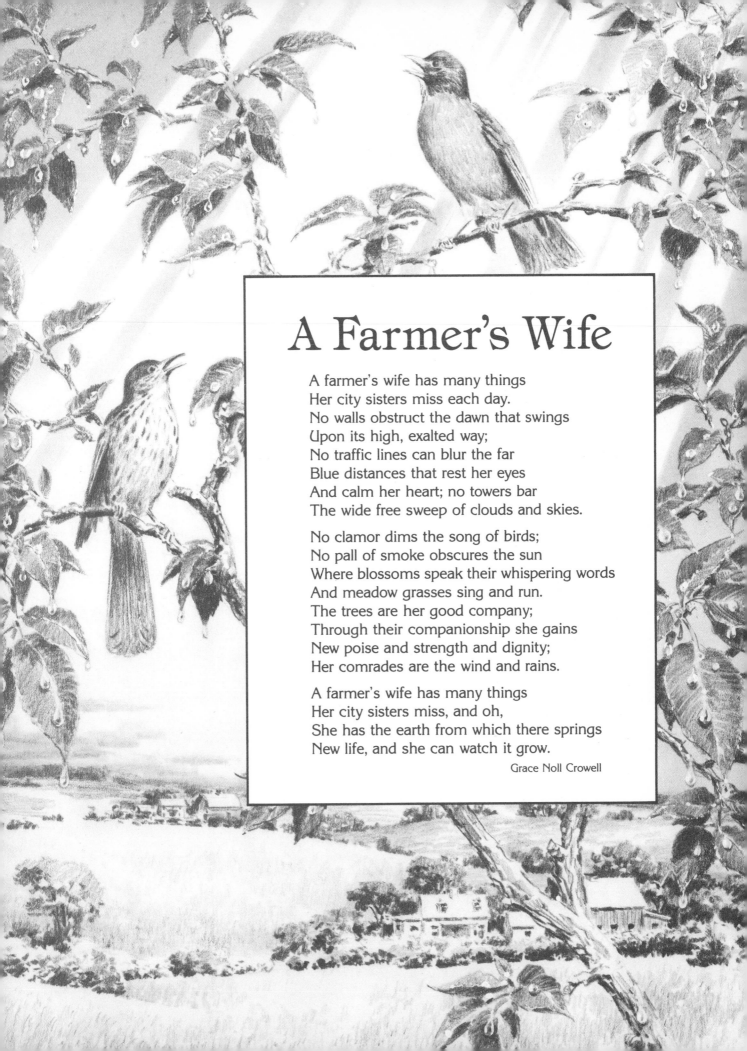

A Farmer's Wife

A farmer's wife has many things
Her city sisters miss each day.
No walls obstruct the dawn that swings
Upon its high, exalted way;
No traffic lines can blur the far
Blue distances that rest her eyes
And calm her heart; no towers bar
The wide free sweep of clouds and skies.

No clamor dims the song of birds;
No pall of smoke obscures the sun
Where blossoms speak their whispering words
And meadow grasses sing and run.
The trees are her good company;
Through their companionship she gains
New poise and strength and dignity;
Her comrades are the wind and rains.

A farmer's wife has many things
Her city sisters miss, and oh,
She has the earth from which there springs
New life, and she can watch it grow.

Grace Noll Crowell

My Neighbor's Yard

My neighbor's grass is prim and neat;
Mine, scuffed and trampled by small feet.
Her garden boasts fine flower beds;
Mine, wind-ruffled yellow heads.
(And is it strange a mother holds
These lovelier than marigolds?)
Her garden paths are low-box-bordered;
Mine, toy strewn, mud-pie disordered.

(What is she thinking when she scans
The kiddy cars, the pattypans?)
Both yards have hedges round about;
Mine shuts in what hers shuts out.
Above my children's shouts, a bird
In her shrubbery is heard!
Oh, if my neighbor's yard but had
One little sun-browned noisy lad!

Ethel Romig Fuller

A House
I Know

I've never walked the curving path
To a certain house I know,
But I am sure it's a happy house.
Mine was like it long ago—
A sandbox filled with toys,
Blue aprons on the line,
Yellow roses by the dooryard,
Windowpanes that shine,

Pink hollyhocks out back,
A lilac bush in bloom,
A curtain blowing, ruffly white,
To grace a sunny room.

And even if I never call,
This family's heart I know
Is warm and true and happy;
Their house has told me so.

Lucille Crumley

Wild Flowers

The wild flowers bloom beside the road—
So often hidden there,
All tucked away within the day
Beneath the blue skies fair,
A lovely scented violet
So shy within the grass
And daisies small, not seen at all
As folks would quickly pass.

The wild flowers blossom everywhere,
A tender gift from God,
By country lane, in springtime rain
Where little feet shall tread;
And little hearts delight to find
Each tiny golden head;
Forever sought, it matters not
They grace no flower bed.

The dandelions thrill them so,
Profusely growing wild.
Though you and I might pass them by,
They're loved by every child;
They pick a precious big bouquet
Within their tiny hand
And love to share the beauty fair
Of wild flowers of our land.

Garnett Ann Schultz

Sweets for Mother

Napoleons

Makes 10.
Preparation Time: 45 minutes.

Easy Puff Pastry
Custard Filling
Chocolate Icing

Prepare puff pastry dough and Custard Filling. Preheat oven to 425°. Spread puff pastry on greased 10 x 15-inch jelly-roll pan. Prick with tines of fork at ¼-inch intervals. Bake 12 minutes. Cool. Cut into thirds, forming 3 5 x 10-inch pieces. Spread one rectangle with half of Custard Filling; top with second rectangle of dough and spread with remaining filling. Top with remaining rectangle. Prepare Chocolate Icing and spread over top. Chill until serving time.

Easy Puff Pastry

Makes 8 to 10 napoleons.
Preparation Time: 1 hour, 15 minutes.

1 cup butter
1½ cups flour
½ cup dairy sour cream

Cut butter into flour in bowl until completely blended. Stir in sour cream to form dough. Chill 1 hour. Roll out into size desired for napoleons *or* pastries.

Custard Filling

1 3¾-ounce package instant French vanilla pudding mix
1¼ cups milk
1 cup whipping cream, whipped

Prepare pudding mix according to package directions using 1¼ cups milk, stirring until thickened. Chill. Fold in whipped cream.

Chocolate Icing

¼ cup butter *or* margarine
1½ ounces unsweetened chocolate
⅛ teaspoon salt
1½ cups confectioners' sugar
2 tablespoons milk
1 teaspoon vanilla

Melt butter and chocolate in saucepan over low heat. Add salt and confectioners' sugar; beat until smooth. Beat in milk and vanilla.

Cherry-Raspberry Pie

Makes 6 servings.
Preparation Time: 1 hour, 30 minutes.

1 9-inch double piecrust
3 cups pitted red tart cherries, fresh *or* canned
1 pint fresh raspberries *or* 1 10-ounce package frozen raspberries, thawed and drained
1 cup granulated sugar
¼ cup flour
2 tablespoons butter
1 egg yolk
2 tablespoons water
Granulated sugar

Preheat oven to 425°. Combine cherries, raspberries, sugar and flour in a large bowl; toss gently. Spoon into bottom crust; dot with butter. Prepare a lattice top crust and place on top of filling. Mix egg yolk and water; brush over lattice. Sprinkle with sugar. Bake 30 to 35 minutes or until crust is golden. Cool on rack.

Flowering May

The apple blossoms pink and white
Perfume the month of May
Across the meadows, emerald green,
That dance in bright array.

The lilac trees in loveliness
Bloom purple everywhere
And send their pungence far and wide
With fragrance through the air.

The dandelions yellow-gold
Adorn the fields around
And turn their faces toward the sun
Where rays of warmth are found.

The violets so sweet and blue
Peek out from neath the trees
And smile with dainty tenderness
Among protective leaves.

The tulips and the garden flowers
Are blooming oh so fast,
And everything is bursting out;
Now spring has come at last.

Gertrude Rudberg

Only a Housewife?

Only a housewife?
Oh, no, it can't be!
She's an artist, a painter,
A soul bright and free,
A faith and a courage
Through dark tragic days,
A hope still undaunted,
The sun's brightest rays.

Only a housewife—
She's a builder of dreams
With plans for tomorrow
In commonplace things,
A sonnet of beauty,
A song to impart,
A soul filled with living,
A prayer in her heart.

Only a housewife—
Contentment is there
With keen understanding,
A peace shining fair;
Artist, poet and builder,
A mother so proud,
Hers is the task
Just the brave are allowed.

She's the strength of the household,
With goodness untold,
And hers is the glory
That never grows old.
A better tomorrow,
'Tis this she shall own,
Not only a housewife—
The foundation of home.

Garnett Ann Schultz

A Mother's Talent

I've watched her mold with expert gentle care
And paint and fire her precious pottery.
How grand to find she has a talent rare—
A talent of the finest artistry!
I've watched her raise a family so fine
With loving care, and that, too, is an art.

To mold good lives requires a gift divine,
With careful work and planning from the start.
Just as a potter fashions from the clay
A rigid, useful pot we're proud to own,
A parent, with God's help, can find the way
To raise a child with strength to stand alone.
There is no higher calling on the earth
Than molding lives of character and worth.

Darlene Bowden

In a Garden

Here among the budding flowers,
I have known such happy hours,
Learned new lessons every day,
Looked at things a different way.
Values change when you are set
In a patch of mignonette.

Looking in a pansy's face,
I have found a sweeter grace,
In the still heart of a rose
All the peace that nature knows,
From a clump of marigold
Something for my heart to hold.

In this little patch of ground,
There is something clean and sound.
Every spade of soil you turn,
There is something new to learn.
Here amid the sun and rain,
I have found myself again.

Edna Jaques

I'm in
Love with You

Your eyes are always shining
Like the sun a-getting up
When the dew is all a-sparkling
On the golden buttercup;

And your lips, forever smiling
Like a radiant spring day
When the wind is softly sighing
And our hearts are light and gay;

And your cheeks with roses blooming
Like a flower garden fair
When the blossoms, in the morning,
Scatter perfume on the air;

And your voice so soft and mellow
Always thrills me through and through;
All the world, with me, is saying,
"Darling, I'm in love with you."

Justin L. Patterson

A Mother's Treasure

Baby's outgrown dresses,
Saved by loving hands,
Folded with a teardrop,
Mother understands.

Babyhood's a moment
Wishing will not stay,
Leaving poignant memories
Saved and tucked away.

Dan A. Hoover

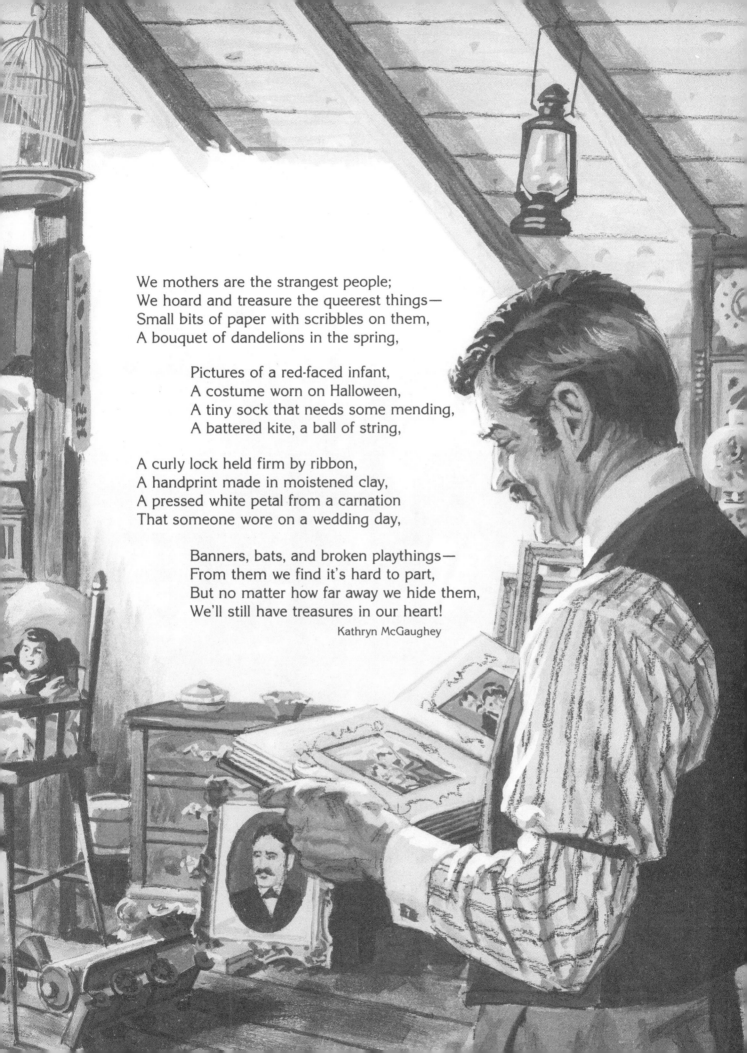

We mothers are the strangest people;
We hoard and treasure the queerest things—
Small bits of paper with scribbles on them,
A bouquet of dandelions in the spring,

Pictures of a red-faced infant,
A costume worn on Halloween,
A tiny sock that needs some mending,
A battered kite, a ball of string,

A curly lock held firm by ribbon,
A handprint made in moistened clay,
A pressed white petal from a carnation
That someone wore on a wedding day,

Banners, bats, and broken playthings—
From them we find it's hard to part,
But no matter how far away we hide them,
We'll still have treasures in our heart!

Kathryn McGaughey

A Mother's Day Blessing

A mother's gift of laughter,
A mother's gift of love,
A mother's gift of hope
Are blessings from above.

Her cheerful smile that dries a tear,
Her kindly words that soothe a fear
Are why I'm thankful when I say,
"God bless you, Mother, on your day."

Betty J. Silconas

ACKNOWLEDGMENTS

A FARMER'S WIFE by Grace Noll Crowell. Used by permission of Reid Crowell. FAMILY TREE by Alice Joyce Davidson. From REFLECTIONS OF LOVE by Alice Joyce Davidson, Copyright © 1983 by Alice Joyce Davidson. Published by Fleming H. Revell Company. Used by permission. MOTHER'S WORK by Cora Lindsey Field. From IN PRAISE OF MOTHERS, Copyright 1947 and 1939 by J. Harold Gwynne. JUST A MOTHER by Lorraine Halli. First published in SCOPE, May 1979. Reprinted by permission of the author. LILACS by Essie L. Mariner. From her book: ENCOUNTERED. Used by permission of Jennings W. Mariner. MOTHER (on title page) by Margaret E. McCaul. From her book: REFLECTIONS IN MINIATURE. Copyright © by Margaret E. McCaul and Armour Home. Reprinted with permission. THE GREATEST GIFT by Phyllis C. Michael. Copyright 1964 by Phyllis C. Michael in POEMS FROM MY HEART, Zondervan Publishing House. APRIL AND MAY by Anne Robinson from SUNG UNDER THE SILVER UMBRELLA. Reprinted by permission of Anne Robinson and the Association for Childhood Education International, 3615 Wisconsin Avenue, N.W., Washington, D.C. 20016. Copyright © 1935 by the Association. IT IS MAY by Pearl Lange Schuler. From MY HEART SINGS, Copyright © 1956 by Pearl Lange Schuler. FOR MOTHER'S DAY by Grace V. Watkins. Previously published in YOUTH. Used by permission of the author. CHERRY-RASPBERRY PIE; EASY PUFF PASTRY; NAPOLEONS from: PIES AND PASTRIES COOKBOOK by Naomi Arbit and June Turner. Copyright © 1982 by Naomi Arbit and June Turner. Published by Ideals Publishing Corporation. Our sincere thanks to the following authors whose addresses we were unable to locate: Julia S. Anderson for THE ROSE I GREW; Minnie Roberts Dreesen for SPRING; Mrs. Romig C. Fuller for MY NEIGHBOR'S YARD by Ethel Romig Fuller; Justin L. Patterson for I'M IN LOVE WITH YOU; Hester Suthers for A MOTHER'S SONG.

COLOR ART AND PHOTO CREDITS
(in order of appearance)

Front and back cover, Fred Sieb; inside front and back cover, Colour Library International (USA) Limited; Window Garden, Fred Sieb; Mother's Song, Gerald Koser; Lilacs in Spring, Gerald Koser; Fireweed at Colorado Trout Lake, Sheep Mountain, Ed Cooper; Church in the Vale, near Ontario, Wisconsin, Ken Dequaine; Beacon Hill Park, Victoria, Vancouver, British Columbia, Ed Cooper; The Rose Mother Grew, Colour Library International (USA) Limited; Backyard Garden, Harold M. Lambert; Garden Gazebo, Alpha Photo Associates; Rose Garden, Harold M. Lambert; Fence Lines, Donald S. Henning; Rose for mother, H. Armstrong Roberts; Mayflower bouquet, Colour Library International (USA) Limited; Motherly Love, Bob Taylor; Kitten in Clay Pot, Robert Cushman Hayes; Bellingrath Gardens, Theodore, Alabama, Fred Sieb; Family Outing, Freelance Photographers Guild; Blossoming Valley, near Bangor, Wisconsin, Ken Dequaine; Girl picking dandelions, H. Armstrong Roberts; Sweets for Mother, Gerald Koser; Blossoming May, Hampfler Studios; Oregon pansies, Botanical Garden, Ed Cooper; Rock garden, Josef Muench; Out for a stroll, H. Armstrong Roberts; Gift of Love, Gerald Koser; Children in field of flowers, H. Armstrong Roberts.

Celebrate the Beauty of Friendship . . .

The distinctive Friendship issue offers a rich array of poetry, quotations, artwork and photography to celebrate the beauty of friendship. A selection of writings of best-loved poet Henry van Dyke offers an inspirational view of friendship. Norman Rockwell's painting *Little Spooners* is featured in this issue. A companion article by Dr. Donald Stoltz provides an insight into the life of this renowned artist. Readers will welcome a portrayal of the joys of hometown living and the loveliness of summer gardens as well as (the return of) familiar poems such as "The Village Blacksmith" and "The House by the Side of the Road." Memorial Day, graduation, Flag Day and other traditional, well-loved events of this time of year are saluted in prose, poetry and photography.

Ideals is a wonderful way to share the beautiful world we live in with our family and friends. A subscription can provide a wonderful gift to remind our friends that we are thinking of them on at least eight special occasions throughout the year. Isn't there a loved one, a cherished friend or shut-in who might appreciate a subscription to Ideals as much as you do?